Photographs
© Éric Chauché pages 108, 109 t and br, 110, 111 t and b;
© Corbis pages 28, 29, 30, 31, 35, 39, 113.

Design and creation: GRAPH'M

ISBN: 2-7528-0016-9
Publisher code: T00016

Copyright registration: October 2004
Printed in Singapore by Tien Wah Press

www.fitwaypublishing.com
Fitway Publishing
12, avenue d'Italie - 75627 Paris cedex 13

extreme **S**ports

surfing

grégory maubé
photographs sylvain cazenave

fitway
publishing

The Australian, Layne Beachley, female world champion and six times Australian champion, thinks nothing of competing against the most elite *male* surfers (most recently in the Energy Australia Open).

Contents

THE ORIGINS OF SURFING
Origin and decline   10
The first age   10
The dark days   14

The renaissance of surfing
The pioneers of modern surfing   18
The father of modern surfing:
Duke Kahanamoku   20
Tom Blake: research and development   26

The adolescence of rebellious surfing
Starting to spread   28
The Malibu gang   36
The *Endless Summer* phenomenon:
the quest for the perfect wave   38

The 80s and 90s:
economic and cultural boom years
The beginnings of professionalism   40
The charismatic figures of the 1980s   42
Kelly Slater and the New School   52
Surfing and style: Joël Tudor   62

Tomorrow's horizons and challenges

Bigwave riding 66

The tow-in 72

In search of the new wave: wave pools and seiches 76

WATER TALES:
SYMBOLIC SURFING FIGURES

Mickey 'Da Cat' Dora: the rebel surfer 82

Robert 'Nat' Young, the 'Animal' 84

Gerry Lopez, 'Mr Pipeline' 86

Wayne 'Rabbit' Bartholomew: the beginnings of
professional surfing 88

Tom Curren: competition and aestheticism 90

Christian Fletcher: the free surfer 92

Kelly Slater: the living god 94

Andy Irons: the Hawaiian relief 96

Rell Sunn: queen of Makaha 98

Lisa Andersen: surfing and parity 100

ENVIRONMENT AND TECHNIQUE

The surfer–globetrotter's guide 102

How does it work? 106

Made by surfers for surfers 108

The relationship between man and nature 112

Surfrider Foundation 114

Conclusion 116

Surfing terminology 118
Further information 120

The origins
of surfing

The **first age**

Like the marathon, surfing is one of the oldest sporting or artistic disciplines in the world. But of course it is impossible to give any precise date for the first time when human beings ventured on to a surfboard. The moment when the first surfer rode mankind's first wave is a magical image for surfers everywhere in the world, but unfortunately no photographer was there to capture it. There are only a few wall paintings and other forms of tribal legend to inspire our unconscious minds and feed our 'genetic heritage' as surfers.

Although several geographical areas (Peru, Senegal, Tahiti and Hawaii), independently of each other, were the playgrounds for this ancestral culture in its infancy, historians and surfers agree that the roots of modern surfing were Polynesian. The history of the settlement of the Polynesian archipelagos would seem to indicate that they were populated by a mixture of two ethnic groups, Caucasian and Mongolian, around 2000 BC. This long history, synonymous with the first age of surfing, was responsible for these migrants' profound sensitivity to and deep respect for the ocean.

In 1777 Captain James Cook was the first European to study at Tahiti and then describe a surfing scene (wave-riding). The notes and accounts of British and French explorers describe natives riding the waves on outrigger canoes or on small boards *(païpo)*. The surfer enjoyed and repeated the procedure to the point of exhaustion, waiting for the wave, rowing fiercely and riding it out each time. There was a considerable degree of cultural shock, for this tribal and ancestral tradition was equivalent to pagan idleness and fickleness in the eyes of these highly puritanical navigators. The native Polynesian was a pleasure-lover and devoted to the ocean. This common feature of Tahiti and Hawaii was the result of cultural exchanges that had developed during the long voyages between the two archipelagos. Surfing, or *He'e Nalu* in Hawaiian, was celebrated as an ardent encounter with nature practised by everyone without any restrictions on age. Depending on circumstances surfing might be a royal, divine or merely playful pursuit.

In the 18th century European civilisation did not think of the ocean in the same way. When the natives of Polynesia

Opposite and on the following double pages: *Although the origin of surfing is ascribed to several geographical areas – Peru, Senegal and Tahiti – the Hawaiian archipelago conjures up the greatest number of images of this tribal and ancestral pursuit.*

were developing a tradition of coastal navigation Europeans were developing ocean-going navigation, designed for deep waters and not for coastal trading. Neither their needs nor their relations with nature were the same. The Polynesians understood and tamed the ocean, riding the waves of the coastline. With less extensive maritime knowledge and a more functional approach to the ocean, Europeans remained frightened of the vast expanse of the seas.

Even though fragments of Hawaiian boards, several centuries old, are on show in the Bishop Museum in Honolulu, it is still impossible to date the first occasion when a human being ventured on to a board. All we can do is to guess that the idea of using a wave to return to the shore is attributable to some Hawaiian or Tahitian coastal fisherman who had gone out on an outrigger or a similar device. But what process of experimentation led to the making of the first board after that?

The **dark days:** the decline of **Hawaiian traditions**

James Cook was aware that his discovery sounded the death-knell of Polynesian civilisation and traditions. Early 19th century Hawaiian society consisted of several independent tribes and found itself unable to resist European cultural, political and religious imperialism.

Fascinated as they were by Polynesian culture the first 'naturalist' explorers, under the influence of Calvinist theories (rampant in Europe at the time of the industrial revolution), nevertheless decided that Polynesian civilisation was inferior to their own. The colonisation period ushered in the decline of Hawaiian traditions, way of life and especially of the pastime of surfing. Admittedly, the European presence made it possible to unite the islands of the archipelago, but at the same time rendered obsolete the *Kapu*, the system of rules and prohibitions by which 'primitive' Hawaiian society was governed. This ancestral system was more than symbolic for it served to link the different Hawaiian cultural and religious traditions together.

Puritan Christian values led to the eradication of nudity, sexual freedom, idleness and the leisure pursuits of communal life. The missionaries converted the inhabitants, not without violence, to the supposedly healthy religious and cultural values of greater Europe. Thereafter surfing, swimming, ritual dancing and all pursuits devoid of any economic interest were forbidden. Nudity was an obstacle to the virtues of modern society and so wearing clothes became obligatory. This requirement led to nothing less than a cultural split. It emphasised the infiltration of the western world and the dependent condition of Hawaiian society. The inhabitants had no resources for making clothes and had to increase production in order to exchange fruit and fish products for manufactured textiles. The entire system of values and traditional crafts collapsed: economic logic condemned the easygoing life and the pursuit of leisure.

Finally the colonists brought a much worse plague with them from the ports of Europe: infectious illnesses and sexually transmitted diseases. They wreaked havoc among a non-immunised people and, within a century, had caused the disappearance of 90% of the indigenous population.

In 1893, after the annexation of the archipelago by the United States, few Hawaiians were still practising the *He'e Nalu*. Labour, 'good manners' and religious prohibitions prevented the handing down of the sport of kings. The secrets of board making and preparation disappeared together with the traditions. Surfing was practised clandestinely. Yet not so long before then, an entire village would have come together on the water to celebrate the arrival of a fine swell.

The last years of the 19th century constituted a gloomy time for surfing. It became a rare sight glimpsed occasionally on Oahu, Maui or Kauai.

The **pioneers** of **modern** surfing

The decline in the number of missionaries and the presence of tourist potential on Hawaii favoured the rebirth of surfing at the beginning of the 20th century. Several iconic figures share the honour of initiating this renewal with regard to knowledge, practice and promoting the ancient discipline. George Freeth is considered to be the pioneer surfer of the modern era (in 1908 he was giving demonstrations in California) but Alexander Hume Ford, an American journalist, was the instigator and above all else the architect of this renewal. With the support of the famous novelist and explorer Jack London he founded the first surfing club in history, the Outrigger Canoe and Surfboard Club, at Waikiki. Even though tribal traditions had been forgotten to some extent, surfing was still an enjoyable discipline in perfect harmony with nature. Waikiki beach became the epicentre of this renaissance and brought to popular notice the man who, it is universally agreed, was the undisputed father of modern surfing and its most effective spokesman: Duke Kahanamoku.

The Bishop Museum of Honolulu is full of tribal vestiges and other relics such as chants and mural paintings of the traditional practice of He'e Nalu.

DUKE'S
CANOE CLUB
WAIKIKI

The **father** of modern surfing: Duke Kahanamoku

For a lot of surfers Duke Paoa Kahinu Mokoe Hulikohola Kahanamoku, aka Duke (the title given to his father by the Duke of Edinburgh on an official visit to Hawaii), is the father of modern surfing. Born on the island of Oahu in 1890, Duke spent his entire childhood close to Waikiki beach. Baptised in the ocean in accordance with Polynesian ancestral rites he was an experienced waterman from his earliest years. At 10 he left school to enjoy life as a beach boy, a term which at that time did not have all its present-day connotations. He and his band of friends of the *hau tree* (a tree totem on Waikiki beach) formed the core of what was to become the *Hui Nalu,* the most representative surfing and swimming club in Hawaiian history.

His daily practice of aquatic disciplines (bodysurfing, swimming, skindiving, surfing, and canoeing) gave him an athlete's body. In 1912 he was the first Hawaiian to win an Olympic medal (100 metres freestyle). A gold medallist, he failed to rediscover his form after World War I, coming second to the young Johnny Weissmüller ('Tarzan') in the 100 metres at the 1924 Olympics.

On his trips abroad the Duke usually carried a surfboard in his luggage. He communicated his enthusiasm for surfing in the form of demonstrations all over the world. From southern California in 1912, via Freshwater, Australia in 1915 (a real culture shock for Australian swimmers) and onwards, immense crowds came to see the phenomenon. He even popularised surfing as an effective means of beach lifesaving, demonstrating this most effectively in 1925 when he participated in the rescue of 12 shipwrecked people in California.

Duke Kahanamoku still watches over 'his' Waikiki beach. His statue invites tourists and passers-by to share in the pleasures of the beach and surfing: Aloha spirit.

Each international visit (to the Olympics or to exhibitions) was an opportunity to include his board in his luggage and to spread the values of Hui Nalu, *the most famous of surfing clubs.*

His growing fame attracted Hollywood. In the films which helped to make him increasingly well known, his roles were as Polynesian chiefs, Aztecs or native Americans. In 1948 he was even cast as John Wayne's enemy in *The Wake of the Red Witch*.

He made a huge contribution to modern surfing. Apart from his technical discoveries, especially on big waves, he was the foremost ambassador for the sport throughout the world. He upheld ancestral traditions and respect for the ocean. His media appearances following the Olympic Games and his Hollywood roles also enabled him to communicate his passionate enthusiasm for surfing and the entire spiritual and metaphysical dimension which surfing still conveys today.

PAUL STRAUCH, JR.   JOEY CABELL   THE DUKE   FRED HEMMINGS   BUTCH VAN ARTSDALEN

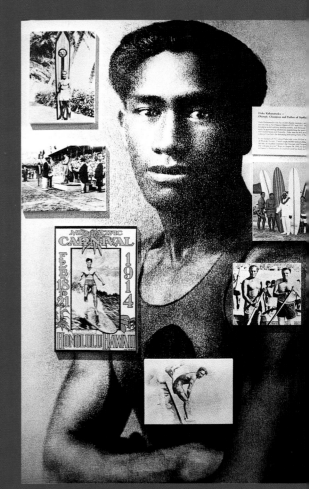

Between exhibitions in swimming pools and Olympic swimming competitions, the Duke was the main ambassador for the rebirth of He'e Nalu at the beginning of the 20th century.
Duke Kahanamoku was a high-class sportsman, a film actor and a figure in local politics. For all surfers everywhere he remains the father of modern surfing and a Hawaiian legend.

Tom Blake:
research and
development

Although the Duke was largely responsible for making surfing popular internationally, Tom Blake deserves to be called the first modern surfer. This ace swimmer and waveriding artist was also a brilliant inventor: he introduced the first hollow surfboards; fins or skegs; a prototype surf leash; waterproof camera housing and the first aquatic photographs; and the sailing surfboard (the first windsurfer). In addition he revolutionised water-rescue techniques by utilising the lifeguard torpedo buoy, for example.

He became a legendary figure following the publication of *The Uncommon Journey of a Pioneer Waterman.* He spread surfing knowledge and culture as well as popularising its practice.

Finally, in 1926 Tom Blake was the first to discover and then to surf the Malibu wave, California, which became world-famous thereafter.

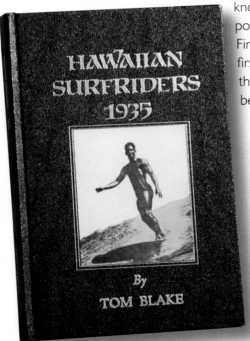

Tom Blake published and described his vision and the development of his relationship with nature under the influence of Hawaiian culture as somewhere between spiritual encounter and initiation rite.

Starting
to spread

Modern surfing and its development as a popular sport is heavily indebted to the Hawaiian pioneers, George Freeth and Kahanamoku. At the beginning of the 20th century, mainly on Waikiki beach, surfriding was a less clandestine and anonymous pursuit than it had been when subject to missionary control. Nevertheless, from the 1920s onwards the Californian craze was a major cause of surfing's popularisation on an international scale. California was the shopwindow of an increasingly dominant USA and surfing there became one of the symbols of the American Way of Life. Not only the closeness of Hollywood and its film industry, but also the quality of the surfing spots all along the Pacific Coast Highway made California the capital of the fashions and trends of surfing culture in the second half of the 20th century. Although surfing spread along the entire West Coast it was Malibu, like Waikiki formerly, that became the epicentre and the main attraction of the Californian surfing community for several decades.

From the 1920s onwards, California became the capital of surfing culture. Malibu beach was the epicentre of all new trends.

California is the
shop-window State of
the USA and symbolises
the American way of life.
Initially, the values of sea,
surf and sun, of the freedom
and anti-conformism
associated with surfing culture
were marginalised,
but eventually a whole section
of American youth were
drawn. They also became a
major resource of the media
and, of course, of Hollywood.

*Above, opposite and on following double
page: Surfing culture invaded Californian society
and influenced the American pursuit of success.
In Hawaii and on the North Shore
(the Backdoor-Pipeline beach is to the right)
the challenge of bigwave riding is always on offer.*

A STOMPLOAD OF TWISTERRIFIC SURF SWINGS!!

DEL-FI RECORDS

THE LIVELY ONES

HANG FIVE!!!
THE BEST OF THE LIVELY ONES

DEL-FI CD 9004

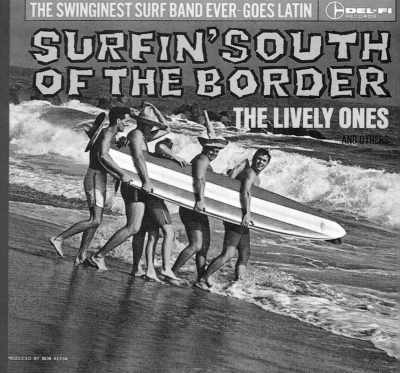

THE SWINGINEST SURF BAND EVER—GOES LATIN

DEL-FI RECORDS

SURFIN' SOUTH OF THE BORDER

THE LIVELY ONES
AND OTHERS

PRODUCED BY BOB KEENE

DELP 1240

WIPE OUT!
THE IMPACTS

DEL-FI RECORDS

DLP 1234

24 OF THE GREATEST SURFIN' HITS!

DEL-FI

WILD SURF!

THE LIVELY ONES • DAVE MYERS AND THE SURFTONES • THE CENTURIONS • THE IMPACTS • THE SENTINALS • AND MORE!

DEL-FI

BIG SURF HITS

artists
THE LIVELY ONES
THE SURF STOMPERS
THE IMPACTS
THE SENTINALS
DAVE MYERS AND THE SURFTONES
THE SURF MARIACHIS
THE CENTURIANS

tunes
SURF RIDER
HILLBILLIE SURF
ORIGINAL SURFER STOMP
GREEN ONIONS
WIPE OUT
BLUE SURF
BIG SURF
MOMENT OF TRUTH
CHURCH KEY
UNDERTOW
WATERMELON MAN
BULLWINKLE P. II

DEL-FI RECORDS

12 SWINGIN' TUNES FOR THE TUFFEST OF BUNNIES

DEL-FI RECORDS

SURFER, GIRL
THE SENTINALS

A BOB KEENE PRODUCTION

DEL-FI RECORDS

KFWB'S BATTLE OF THE SURFING BANDS!

THE LIVELY ONES
CHALLENGERS ■ SENTINALS ■ IMPACTS
CHARADES ■ RHYTHM KINGS
DAVE MYERS & SURFTONES
JIM WALLER & DELTAS ■ THE BISCAYNES
THE SOUL KINGS
THE BRUCE JOHNSTON BAND

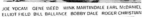
JOE YOCAM   GENE WEED   WINK MARTINDALE   EARL McDANIEL
ELLIOT FIELD   BILL BALLANCE   BOBBY DALE   ROGER CHRISTIAN

Produced by Bob Keene

DFLP 1235

The Malibu **Gang**

At the end of World War II, two Malibu surfers, Bob Simmons and Gard Chapin, discovered a new way of making surfboards using fibreglass and resin. Simmons' board applied findings gained in scientific and military studies of aircraft-wing aerodynamics to an aspect of civilian life, and revolutionised surfing practice. He introduced this technical revolution all along the Californian coastline against a background of petty rivalry between the supporters of neighbouring surfing spots, so its assimilation wasn't as widespread as it might have been.

The influence of Malibu beach, the capital of the new trends, spread all over the world. In the 1950s Mickey Dora and Mickey Munoz were at the very heart of this bubbling enthusiasm. Mickey Dora, the anti-conformist apostle of free surfing, characterised the surfer as a marginal individual in American society. For a long time, according to the conventions of the American Way of Life and consumer society, the surfer was looked upon as a parasite, as a beach bum in fact. Like James Dean and Marlon Brando, Mickey Dora was a symbolic rebel in a puritanical and conservative society.

The influence of Malibu is still with us. Despite the ways in which it has developed technologically and culturally, the ethos of surfing is still innovative when set against the spirit of the age. You could say that the golden age of Malibu beach laid the foundations of modern surfing culture in a realm somewhere between sheer pleasure-seeking and ultimate freedom.

Below: Before becoming the iconic setting of the TV series Baywatch, *Malibu beach was marked by its past of magical surfing sessions and the escapades of its beach boys.*

Opposite:
Close to Santa Barbara in the 1980s, Tom Curren was the charismatic figure and stylistic mentor of Californian surfing.

The *Endless Summer* phenomenon: the **quest** for the **perfect wave**

Fashion led Hollywood to make surfing a topic of several films, but none of them really managed to attract the entire surfing community. In 1964 Bruce Brown made *Endless Summer,* a film which would affect a number of generations and remain a definite benchmark. Quite apart from the spirited production and the quality of actors Mike Hyson and Robert August, *Endless Summer* represented a decisive turning-point in surfing culture and was a source of inspiration for nomadism, mystical travel and cultural cross-breeding.

This quest for a never-ending summertime took Bruce Brown and his production team on a tour of discovery to Senegal, Ghana, Australia, New Zealand and Tahiti. He was the first to go to St. Francis Bay, South Africa, and the virgin waves of nearby Jeffrey's Bay/'J Bay' (now South Africa's most famous surfing spot) still furnish mythical images for surfers around the world.

In 1995 Bruce Brown made *Endless Summer II* at St. Francis Bay and once again offered a lavish portrayal of travelling around the world in search of the ultimate wave, of new encounters and of exchanges of human experience.

Above:
A typical Landes beach scene during the filming of The Endless Summer II, *Bruce Brown's second cult movie.*
Opposite:
Poster showing the immortal image of the endless summer and the quest for the perfect wave.

"CHILLS AND SPILLS CROWD THE SCREEN.
LEAVES A VIEWER BREATHLESS."
Time Magazine

"A PERFECT MOVIE."
The New Yorker

"BREATHTAKING! SWEEPING AND EXCITING."
Newsweek

The Endless Summer

A true motion picture about surfing.
Filmed in Africa, Australia, New Zealand, Tahiti, Hawaii and California.
A BRUCE BROWN FILM IN COLOR
Distributed by Cinema V

The beginnings of professionalism

The film *Endless Summer* was the catalyst for the new surfing spirit: travel and freedom. What with *Surfer Magazine* (first issued 1960), various surf films and the wanderings of globetrotting beach bums, the spread of surfing around the world was contagious.

Hotdogging Australians, initiated into new moves by Nat Young, revolutionised surfing when faced with small to average sets. Boards became shorter; more radical and varied manoeuvres were adopted: the tube, roller and cutback became compulsory forms.

In bigwave riding the revelation of the North Shore (Sunset, Waimea, and Pipeline) waves gave the island of Oahu the status of surfing capital, as it still is today. Every winter the world surfing elite just has to be there. Gerry Lopez, Shaun Thomson, Wayne Lynch and Wayne 'Rabbit' Bartholomew were representative figures in this developing professionalism. With the founding of the ASP and the creation of the Pro Tour, competition surfing acquired a new dimension.

Under the dominating image of the free spirit roving at will, the surfing community has been a remarkable survivor of the hippy period, involuntarily characterised as a kind of happy-go-lucky, pleasure-loving and marginal tribe.

Before climbing above the lip of the wave (as shown in this aerial frontside manoeuvre), surfing turned professional with the founding of the ASP (Association of Surfing Professionals).

The charismatic **figures** of the 1980s

In the early 80s the Australians enjoyed an almost total domination of world surfing. High-spirited, radical and committed, Tom Caroll perfectly symbolised this assertive Aussie culture. Nevertheless it was Tom Curren, a Californian who, by his style and awards (3 titles), most typified professional surfing of the 80s. His sense of harmony on the wave and his attitude, poised as it was between aestheticism and radicalism, formed the basis of modern surfing. Manoeuvres became increasingly spectacular as equipment and technique developed.

The media's infatuation with surfing and the industrial growth of associated brands, which had formerly worked on a craft basis, hastened the popularisation of the sport. The image of the surfer remained closely linked to travel; it was also associated with fluorescent fashion, which meant real commercial success for the surfwear industry. Surfing culture became trendy, urban and market-orientated. Surfshops flourished in big towns and cities and the Pro Tour line-up touched down wherever the effects of media attention seemed to benefit their brand partners.

Scene of the most newsworthy innovations, The North Shore is also the permanent winter destination of leading professionals. Here Tom Carroll executes a cutback frontside on the formidable Pipeline.

Twice world champion, radical surfer and matchless competitor, the Australian Tom Carroll was one of the 'kings' of the Pipe in the 1980s. Here he takes the famous Triple Crown, something he achieved on three occasions.

Gary Elkerton is a powerful and radical surfer,
setting new limits to competitive surfing,
and especially bigwave surfing. He was born
in Australia but fell in love with France and its
beach breaks, setting up there himself in the
late 1980s.

Mark 'Occy' Occhiluppo is the most inventive
and intuitive surfer of this generation.
World champion at the age of 33,
he always places among the top 44 in
competition.

Martin 'Pottz' Potter was one of the precursors of the aerial manoeuvre (opposite), but also an unequalled waverider. His determination and radical approach enabled him to carry off the major title in 1991.

Kelly Slater
and the New School

In the early 90s, its most remarkable representative took the Pro Tour by storm: Kelly Slater. This surfing extra-terrestrial, the spiritual son of Tom Curren, was the inspiration of a new generation of competitors and freesurfers; the influences of this New School clearly came from (street or ramp) skating. Tricks, ollies, air, even the vocabulary of surfing changed. Kelly Slater alone personified this perceptible evolution. His style, technique, ease and six titles made him a reference index for the future. His dominance of the scene was unique until his early retirement, leaving Mark Occhiluppo the opportunity to make his mark at the age of 33.

The street trend gave the surfing industry a second wind by attracting a more urban crowd to the sport. Surfing schools and surfcamps started up everywhere. New means of communication (flying, mobile phones, the Internet, etc.) reduced distances considerably and made that quest for the perfect wave, which surfers often compared to an initiation ceremony, seem almost run of the mill. On the other hand, this technological progress made it possible for lovers of fine waves to enjoy a greater degree of comfort and a wider choice of exceptional spots.

The surfer was no longer a marginalised figure but a member of civil society and no less a citizen of the world. The 90s were also marked by the real beginnings of ecological awareness and the first concerted eco campaigns, since surfers remained passionate defenders of nature.

Kelly Slater is an extra-terrestrial surfer and has carried off six world championships, a record number. His speed, style and inventiveness afford him a pure, spectacular and perfect waveriding technique. He has returned from semi-retirement to become the main inspiration of the New School and the model for most surfers worldwide.

Above: *Rob Machado, Californian surfer and friend of Kelly Slater, was a free surfer in spirit. Nevertheless he was able to master the entire range of New School surfing moves (as this aerial frontside shows).*

Opposite: *Gary Elkerton refuses to end his career willingly. He sets his strength, mastery and commitment against 'the slash' and other New School manoeuvres.*

Previous double page: *Slash, snap, reverse and aerial manoeuvres enriched the range of New School surfers, with Matt Archbold (left-hand page) as their precursor.*

Above and opposite: *Hawaiian surfers scarcely resisted New School surfing techniques. While preserving their unique waveriding sang-froid, especially on big waves, the Hawaiians tried manoeuvres which became basic thereafter: the aerial backside for Bruce Irons (above), and the snap frontside for Noah Johnson (opposite page).*

Following double page: *Kelly Slater was imbued with a missionary zeal. After surpassing Pro Tour riders in class and style he sought to advance the sport by inventing new manoeuvres clearly inspired by skateboarding: this 'rodeo' shows all Kelly's daring and mastery on the Pipeline wave.*

Surfing and style:
Joël Tudor

Since its rebirth, surfing has constantly evolved both technically and socially. Innovations in the shape and the predominance of the shortboard widened the range of possibilities for the surfer. Nevertheless Nat Young, its first promoter, went back to the beginnings and popularised the use of the longboard at the end of the 80s. The longboard represented more than a nod to ancestral traditions. The new emphasis on it enabled the surfing community to rediscover a taste for waveriding and for styles from the past.

Joël Tudor, an exceptionally gifted Californian, was the modern symbol of this renewal. Each of his movements was choreographed like those of a ballet dancer and he represented a far-above average technique, artistic sense and knowledge of the waves. In the war of styles, longboarders aimed at aesthetics and harmony with the wave, whereas shortboarders aspired to constantly increasing radicalism and tricks.

The growing popularity of longboarding alongside third millennium surfing required a truce between these contrasting styles. Joël Tudor was their perfect synthesis because he symbolised the never-ending quest for purity of action and perfect style.

Opposite and following double page:
Like a dancer or matador,
Joel Tudor masters noseriding
(surfing on the 'nose' of the board)
in pure traditional style.

Bigwave riding

Surfing big waves has always proved especially attractive to purists since this pastime, based on a desire for powerful stimulation, releases heaps of adrenalin, heightening the urge for even greater achievement. Legend has it that the Duke himself surfed a big wave of more than 30 feet (10 metres) in Waikiki Bay. But until the end of the 1950s, Makaha was the favourite spot for bigwave riding. The attractiveness of the North Shore (the northern coast of Oahu, on the receiving end of the great Pacific winter swells) was apparent later and Waimea Bay rapidly became the key spot for big surfing. It was normal for all self-respecting bigwave riders to 'shoot a monster' at Waimea. Equipped with guns (tapered bigwave boards making takeoff and high-speed lines less forbidding) they set out to defy the raging seas. Some surfers saw this as an expression of their virility whereas others had a more ritualised approach to the sport. They all acknowledged that bigwave riding was not restricted merely to a courageous contest with the ocean; physical conditioning as well as experience and technique were essential.

An initiation in itself, bigwave riding became global. In the 80s new breaks were discovered and reported in the surfing press: Mavericks in northern California, Todos Santos off Baja, California (western coast of Mexico), Pico Alto in Peru ... Surfing big waves was no longer the preserve of native Hawaiians. Australians, Americans, Brazilians, Tahitians and even Frenchmen like Thierry Domenech and Christian Guevarra joined the closed ranks of bigwave riders.

Since 1965 and the creation of the 'Duke Kahanamoku Invitational Surfing Championships' at Sunset (North Shore) numerous invitationals are held wherever bigwave challenges are found. In homage to the famous Hawaiian bigwave rider, The Eddie Aikau Contest is the most famous. A serious competition, it never starts without swells of

Two competitors in the 'Quicksilver in Memory of Eddie Aikau' competition launch themselves together on to one of the very big waves in Waimea Bay on the North Shore of Hawaii. Dedicated to bigwave rider, Eddie Aikau, who disappeared at sea, this competition can only take place on one single day between 1 December and 28 February (the Hawaiian winter), and then only if the waves are at least 20 feet (6 metres) high.

more than 6 metres and each winter, conditions permitting, sets the cream of the world's bigwave riders against each other.

Finally, however daring he may be, the bigwave rider sometimes reaches his limit. After a certain height (between 20 and 30 feet, 6 and 10 metres, depending on the character of the spots) it is physically impossible to take off normally since the crest engulfs the surfer before the end of takeoff.

This physical constraint was removed not long ago. The emergence of tow-in (towed surfing) at the beginning of the 90s revolutionised the approach to, and the limits of, bigwave riding. With the support of the irrepressible Laird Hamilton, the tow-surfers' group has set itself a new goal: to surf reefs out at sea and defy waves of more than 30 feet (10 metres).

In bigwave riding, the power of the wave is calculated by the size of the lip. Manoeuvres are less radical and arcs are longer.

The tow-in

Herbie Fletcher, a cameraman and longboarder of repute on the North Shore, is the originator of towed surfing. On a winter's day in 1986 he suggested attaching Tom Caroll, Gary Elkerton and Martin Potter to his jet-ski and towing them in to the second Pipeline reef, a wave too hollow to be negotiated normally. The result was awesome: the three colleagues parted on the wave and took lines hitherto unknown on that mythical hollow.

Nevertheless, the emergence of the tow-in in Hawaii was mainly the work of Laird Hamilton and Buzzy Kerbox. Equipped with a zodiac they set out to defy the huge waves of the reefs off Waimea. The zodiac was soon replaced by a scooter and Laird's group tamed the famous spot of Maui henceforth known as 'Jaws'.

The team for each scooter consisted of two surfers who would take over from each other: the driver and the towed surfer. The scooter allowed the surfer to move fast enough on takeoff and when approaching the unfurling area. During the descent the driver stayed as close as possible to the impact area in order to recover the surfer after a fall or on his emergence from the wave. The manoeuvres of both driver and surfer are often critical and both flirt dangerously with the might of the ocean. Contrary to the traditional long, narrow and tapered gun boards (3 metres/10 feet in length) the tow-in, popularised by Laird, is smaller (2.1 metres/7 feet), heavier and fitted with foot straps borrowed from funboards. The weight of the board and its size allow it to withstand and master the turbulence of the unfurling area at high speed.

Every winter the tow-in teams manage to exceed new limits. Other spots, still poorly known or scarcely known at all, become top demonstration locations and the focus of strong emotions. Although Cortes Bank (a reef 150 miles off the Californian coast) is considered to

Since the first years of surfing, riding big waves has been a traditional pursuit and a virtual initiation rite. Defying the fury of the ocean and tackling the great waves that pound the shore is the typical challenge for every self-respecting bigwave rider in search of yet another adrenalin rush.

be the most substantial place in the world never surfed, Teahupoo in Tahiti has become legendary because of Laird Hamilton. The 'Bomb', the 'Millennium', remains the wave that has received the most media attention to date. But until when? Between the requests of sponsors, the media and the quest to surf the biggest wave of all, the tow-surfer has been constantly pushing back the limits. Nowadays outrageous waves are surfed everywhere in the world, from Tasmania to France. Off St-Jean-de-Luz on the Belharra reef, several French teams set out to tackle waves of more than 30 feet (10 metres).

Even if the traditional physical constraints are avoided, tow-in is a practice reserved for an elite of authentic watermen, hardened surfers inured to the worst fall scenarios.

Laird is a leading tow-surfer. He makes his way to every surfing location in the world in search of really big waves and spots where he can demonstrate his special combination of elegance and power.

In search of the new wave: wave pools and seiches

With the dawning of the third millennium of surfing, the sport has two new, more urban-orientated locations for expressive surfing: wave pools and seiches.

There are several wave pools in the world. One of them, the Ocean Dome located near Miyazaki beach, Japan is certainly the most successful. Beneath the protective dome of the sliding roof the atmosphere is tropical with heat, humidity, a sandy beach and vegetation. The wave, created by an ingenious technical process, extends its turquoise waters over some tens of metres above a sandy floor. The size of the wave can vary from 2 to 6 feet (50 cm to 2 metres). The experience is gripping, even if entry charges are high and contact with nature is entirely artificial.

On the other hand seiches in rivers are natural phenomena and add a new element to modern surfing locations. A seiche wave is an oscillation re-ascending the river and is produced by a change in tides at estuary level. The size varies in accordance with the situation, the coefficients, the swell and the wind. Certain experiments tried out in Brazil, classified as 'kamikaze' because of the presence of piranhas or crocodiles, show that a seiche can be over 6 feet (2 metres) high. The wave unfurls on itself, section by section, and advances as a front between the two banks. This practice is under threat because of the increasingly polluted nature of the rivers of this world.

Surfing is continually catching on at new occasions, such as a celebration by a party of friends in the Dordogne, or sound and light displays in Bavaria.

Water tales: symbolic surfing figures

Mickey 'da cat' dora:
the rebel surfer

Initiated to riding following the demonstrations of George Freeth and Duke Kahanamoku, Californian surfers quickly developed a counter-culture. Modern surfing was born in the Hawaiian archipelago but California was responsible for its international popularisation. In this rapidly developing capitalist state, a perfect shop-window for the economic success of the USA, the surfer was thought of as an outsider, an anti-conformist and a rebel: Mickey 'Da Cat' Dora was the perfect incarnation of this character.

Born in Budapest in 1925 he was introduced to surfing and to the spirit of surfing by his stepfather, the famous surfer Gard Chapin. His stormy adolescence gave him a hard, even arrogant, image. He was to the fore in the development of boardmaking (the use of polyurethane foam as a material to replace wood) but remained an inventive and inspired surfer to the full. He treated his board as if it were human and Malibu became the arena for his sporting escapades.

Hollywood called and he played surfing doubles in several films in the 60s. Exerting influence from behind the scenes and getting mixed up in shady business, his cinematic interlude did not destroy his influence on the Malibu surfing community, the epicentre of Californian trends.

He opposed competitive surfing and, in 1967, thought nothing of mooning to the judges and the crowd at the Malibu Invitational Surf Classic. This was to be his last demonstration of protest before myth became one with reality.

Mickey Dora went into voluntary exile in France and travelled to places where surfing was evolving. Between a prison sentence in the 80s and the success of his Da Cat surfboards Mickey Dora continued to embody a rebellious and anti-conformist image. He died in Montecito, California, at the age of 67.

The imprint of his technical know-how is still felt in modern surfing today; he was an inventive master of technique and an advocate of fine style. But he bequeathed much more than that to us: the heritage of the charismatic, nomadic surfer, the symbol of a certain idea of freedom and of the spirit of surfing.

Robert 'Nat' Young, the 'Animal'

Robert Young was born in Sydney and, like many Australians, the beach was his playground. 'Nat' (the nickname he was given because of his resemblance to a little lizard found in the coastal sand) became a competitive surfer at 14, and at 16 he won the title of Senior Champion of Australia.

With George Greenough and Bob McTavish, two of the top Australian shapers, he developed and tested a board of unconventional dimensions, being much smaller and delicate. This revolution proved itself by his first competition wins and was a turning point in modern surfing practice. Whereas the competition surfer was satisfied with following the unfurling wave in an almost linear movement, Nat Young's new board offered him a wider choice of manoeuvres. Now a surfer could take more daring lines and use the power of the wave itself to make increasingly sharp and impressive turns and spins. Quite apart from his own results, Nat Young has breathed a dynamism into Australian surfing which has been known ever since for its robust radicalism and highly aggressive approach.

Throughout his career, Nat Young has never stopped trying to extend his limits and to strive for constant innovation. Awarded a new nickname as 'The Animal', he drags his big carcass to every spot in the world in order to hand on his avant-garde vision of the sport.

Nat has always been a globetrotter. His trips and written accounts of his innovations ensure him constantly growing media coverage. He is a living legend of modern surfing. His ingenious riding technique and visionary nature have made lasting contributions to the development of shortboard surfing.

Finally, he is the father of the renewal of longboard surfing and inspired his worthy successor, Joël Tudor.

Gerry Lopez, 'Mr Pipeline'

For every surfer in the world two terms will always serve to immortalise Gerry Lopez: 'tube' and 'pipeline'.

He was a native of Honolulu who did his first surfing and tube manoeuvres at the Ala Moana spot in the mid-1960s. He was an iconic figure of the shortboard revolution, a mystic practising yoga and other forms of meditation who developed a natural, almost feline, ease in tuberiding. He was the first to use all his arts to elicit the qualities of the dangerous Pipeline break: a still largely avoided spot of the North Shore. His grace, harmony with the water and instinct as a tuberider gave a new dimension to riding this type of water. The tube became this surfer's most successful form of artistic expression and certainly his most intoxicating. Lopez's mystical approach enabled him to operate with something like the aesthetics of a matador, all with a supernatural ease.

He introduced the Lightning Bolt board brand in 1971, and his commitment to and natural performance in tubes, capable of such devastation for surfers, earned him the respect of the international surfing community. He dominated as the pipe surfer of the 70s as, in fact, 'Mr Pipeline'. From 1993 to 1997, competition surfing on the same spot bore his name: the Gerry Lopez Chiemsee Pipe Masters.

A spiritual explorer and indefatigable searcher for the perfect wave, he took part in the first trips organised to Uluwatu (Bali) and stayed for quite a time on his Indonesian wave: G-Land (G for Gerry). Contrary to the Pipeline, a short, radical and intense wave experience, Indonesian waves enabled him to taste the pleasures of almost infinite riding while pursuing his transcendental research in the 'Green Room'.

After several trials for amateur productions this honoured surfer succumbed to another passion: the cinema. He was up there with Arnold Schwarzenegger in *Conan the Barbarian* (he is Conan's Mongolian companion) and, in 1976, he immortalised his distinguished surfing in John Millius' famous surfing film, *Big Wednesday*.

Gerry was always anxious that surfing should continue to develop and constantly tried to perfect his technique. His snowboarding (freeriding) and tow-in experiments on Jaws enabled him to extend his range of techniques with carving, as well as his craving for adrenalin.

He remains a legendary surfer, in particular on account of his perfect reading of the wave and his magical approach to tuberiding in his favourite trial location, the Pipe.

Wayne 'Rabbit' Bartholomew:
the beginnings
of professional surfing

Wayne 'Rabbit' Bartholomew is a pioneer of professional surfing, an iconic figure in surfing and an active member of the ASP (Association of Professional Surfers).

This Australian was born in Snapper Rocks and has his own special location: Kirra (Gold Coast). Legend tells us that the very young Rabbit (a nickname he was given because of his speed on a football pitch) was the surfer who did the most tuberiding or riding the inside of hollow waves. He knows every minute aspect of the Kirra wave. His interminable sessions have given him an astounding tuberiding assurance and style.

He was world champion in 1978 and remained in the world's top five for seven years. His tactical style and form, tested at every challenging spot, make him a formidable competitor. Nevertheless he is still a globetrotting surfer and gives surfing a modern image of travel and freedom.

He has become a coach (Gary Elkerton, Sunny Garcia), a protector of nature (Surf Rider Foundation) and a competition organiser (Kirra). He is currently chair of the ASP. He continues to work for the popularisation of surfing while honouring the ancestral values of the sport: respect for the ocean, cultural encounters and the traveller's quest.

Tom Curren:
competition and aestheticism

Tom Curren was one of the primary figures of surfing in the 1980s. He played an important part in making modern surfing more popular, especially in France.

The son of Pat Curren, a top bigwave rider of the Waimea period, Tom received his training as a boy on the legendary Rincon wave south of Santa Barbara, California. This long, regular wave enabled him to refine his famous roller frontside and unique roundhouse-cutback moves both technically and artistically. He was a radical surfer whose technique and entire aesthetic dimension remain unequalled today.

He is the mythical and iconic figure associated with the Channel Islands brand (shaper: Al Merrick) and, together with Cheyne Horan, he was one of the first surfers to take a genuine interest in the shape of his boards. This interest in shape is indispensable for high-level surfing and allowed him to develop his technique and virtually to perfect it.

He was world amateur champion at Biarritz in 1982 and subsequently carried off three professional world champion titles in 1984, 1985 and 1990. His surfing and charisma marked an entire generation of surfers. His duels with Tom Caroll, Gary Elkerton, Occy (the 'waveriding genius') and Martin Potter ('Pott'z') enlivened competitive surfing in the 80s. His tactical sense and extraordinary wave sensitivity, together with a truly exemplary style, disheartened many of his opponents, especially during his last acquisition of the world title in 1990 (which he won outside the qualifying

conditions: unique in the short history of competitive surfing). He also stands for the end of Australian domination since the founding of the Pro Tour.

He has been resident in France for ten years or so, enjoying the quality of the waves and of everyday life, and has had an immense influence on French surfing. He is the primary inspiration of surfers in the Basque country and the Landes, and his support for the foundation of the European Surf Rider Foundation is an expression of his love and respect for the ocean.

Now Tom Curren is retired, but he still takes part by invitation in a few prestigious competitions. His style, technique and wave sensitivity are as good as ever and he is still able to outdo anyone on a wave.

Between surfing sessions and musical concerts this experienced guitarist continues to satisfy his passion for travel and new encounters with the same determination. His attitude, charisma and incomparable surfing make him one of the most universally acknowledged citizens of the surfing world.

Finally, as a great visionary he was the godfather of the most famous surfer in the world: that living god, Kelly Slater. The most aesthetically magnificent of surfers may be said to have handed the torch on to the most honoured.

Christian Fletcher:
the free surfer

Like Tom Curren, Christian Fletcher has a prominent place in the world surfing annals of the 1980s. Unlike the legendary champion, however, his international fame was not won through competition but through the simplest of surfing modes: free surfing. This is something of a paradox considering that his blossoming media profile accompanied the popularisation of surfing in the 80s and the development of professionalism.

This surfer from San Clemente, California, son of a family of surfers (Herbie, the father, a surfer and producer of surfing films; Nathan, his brother, a multi-specialist in skating-type sports), represents the trash or hardcore variety of surfing. A rebel surfer with either shaved head or long hair, tattoos and piercings, he is an iconic figure of the far-out surfing of the 80s, anti-conformist and evolutionary. His mastery of aerial surfing and his skating and snowboard influences enabled him to express his personality in his radical, atypical riding manoeuvres.

There were no half measures as far as grassroots surfers were concerned: either you worshipped him, or you detested him. Yet no one could accuse him of going along with the spirit of surfing conceived of as freedom and travel, nor of being one of the protagonists of the economic boom of the 80s.

He was made a star by paternalistic audio-visual productions (*Wave Warrior*) and he spearheaded the Astrodeck brand (the non-slip grip). He symbolises the far-out surfer, always pushing the boundaries and aiming higher towards the physical limits of a pursuit, whilst consistently searching for inspiration and innovation. Christian Fletcher is an avant-garde artist of surfing. He has stamped a whole generation of riders with his own imprint. His influence and outsider ethos is as prevalent among surfers as it is among skaters or, more recently, snowboarders. He demonstrates another route to professionalism: that of being paid by brands for surfing and developing his sport.

His major media presence, his awesome contribution to the development of surfing and especially his far-out manoeuvres, place him from now on in the very tight circle of legendary surfers.

Kelly Slater: the living god

Like Michael Jordan in basketball, Pelé in football or Pete Sampras in tennis, Kelly Slater is the top surfer: he has won the most titles, is the most charismatic and gifted and, in short, the best of surfers. There is no superlative we cannot use to describe this authentic living god of modern surfing.

From boyhood, the lad from Cocoa Beach, Florida was proclaimed as the worthy successor of Tom Curren. Now there is nothing in his way. Six times world champion and vice-champion in 2003 (after four years of semi-retirement) he has secured all the records: the youngest world champion at 21, most wins in a single season (seven) and the top awards in competitions and sponsorship. He is rapid, radical and innovative: the extra-terrestrial surfer. Everyone agrees that seeing Kelly Slater surf is to see superbly judged movement, perfect wave-sense and unequalled radicalism. He is head and shoulders above everyone else on the Pro Tour. His opponents are relegated to the category of foils at best.

The iconic figure of the Quiksilver brand since 1990, he presents an ultra-positive image for all the media: that of a brilliant surfer and a handsome, approachable young man. This outstandingly gifted sportsman is supremely versatile. He takes up golf and hey presto! He is unbeatable in the miniature world of surfer–golfers. He plays the guitar and forms a group called *The Surfers* with two friends, the former professionals Rob Machado and Peter King. ACD is already out.

As with Gerry Lopez, Hollywood has looked on him with favour. He has tried the role of actor in the sitcom with the greatest media following in the world: *Baywatch*. His fame extends beyond the mere world of surfing and his relationship with the sultry Pamela Anderson gives him star status. These various extra-surfing successes and his almost stifling attention from the media (the crowds come in their thousands to watch him in competitions) make him inclined to distance himself from the professional world. At 26 he is the youngest semi-retired champion in the history of surfing. When he takes part in a few major competitions he reminds his fans and other competitors that his waveriding is always perfect and that to beat him is a serious challenge. The freedom he has chosen enables him to try out new manoeuvres, to practise tow-in and carving and to develop his control in free surfing.

As with Michael Jordan and his fantastic comeback for the Chicago Bulls, Kelly Slater returned one hundred per cent to the professional circuit in 2003. Feeling that his main competition was centred around a few exceptional surfers like Andy Irons, Taj Burrow and Mick Fanning, his competitive surfing is now taking on another dimension: he is more lively, more aerial and more stylish. His maturity, vitality and ingenuity always enable him to rise above simple good fortune. At 31, Kelly is only the 2003 vice-champion, but more than accruing records, he passionately desires, like Nat Young in his era, to ensure the lasting development of modern surfing.

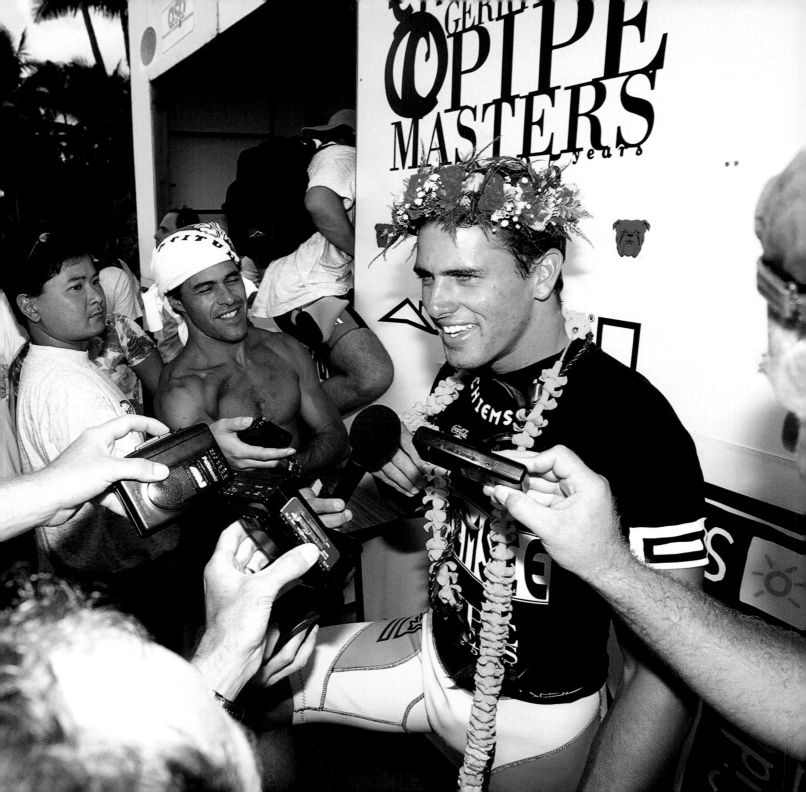

Andy Irons:
the Hawaiian relief

Andy Irons was born on the island of Kauai (Hawaii) in 1978. From a very early age, he and his brother Bruce, younger than Andy by one year, devoted themselves to the ancestral practice for which Hawaii was still the place of all pilgrimages at the end of the 1980s. Even though he was brought up in an idyllic and heavenly environment, his roots didn't stop him participating in American university competitions. His New School approach and his technical ease made him one of the most promising surfers of the Hawaiian school. His victory at HIC Pipeline Proen in 1996 marked the start of his career: at the age of 18 he beat the first Hawaiian world champion, Derek Ho, in the final.

Having qualified for the WCT circuit in 1997, he won his first major competition in 1998 during the OP Pro at Huntington Beach (California). Many observers already saw him as the successor to Kelly Slater, the 'living god'.

After several inconclusive years, which were necessary for him to become hardened to the experiences of competitive surfing, he burst into the limelight by dominating the WCT 2002 Tour (four victories), winning his first title as world champion. His performance was applauded and attracted much attention. Kelly Slater then returned 100 per cent to the circuit in 2003 and the two men locked in a furious *mano a mano*. Andy defeated Kelly in a whirlwind finish at the final test at the 'queen of competitions', the Pipe, and claimed his second consecutive world title.

Andy is on top of the world, and nothing and no one seems to be able to touch him. His competitive qualities, combined with his charisma and style, have made him an extraordinary surfer. Guardian of Hawaiian surfing, he is also one of the spearheads of the New School generation.

At the age of 25, he joined the aristocracy of surfing history, with the same title as his own role-models: Curren, Potter, Occy and Archbolt. Following the Duke, Andy Irons has written one of the best pages in the book of Hawaiian surfing.

Rell Sunn:
queen of Makaha

Like the Duke in the 1920s, throughout her life Rell Sunn contributed to the healthy and traditional popularisation of Hawaiian surfing.

Rell Sunn was born on the island of Oahu and soon became an accomplished waterwoman (longboard, paddle, skin-diving). She was a passionate competitor in the late 1960s and always seemed to take pride of place at important meetings. She was also one of the founders of the first women's Professional Surfing Tour and of the Women's Professional Surfing Association.

Apart from her passion for the pursuit of the gods, so rooted in Polynesian tradition, she took under her wing a number of young Hawaiians who were at a loose end because of the failure of educational or professional aspirations and introduced them to surfing. She was indeed a 'Mother Teresa' of Oahu, and an entire generation of Hawaiian surfers who achieved honours, like Johnny Boy Gomes and Sunny Garcia, owe her an immense debt.

Accordingly, in the mid-70s she invented surfing as a means of social elevation. But her greatest concern was to teach respect for others and for nature.

Her efforts were not restricted to the Hawaiian archipelago alone. In 1986, under the aegis of *Surfer Magazine*, she visited China to impart her wisdom to surfers there. She was a keen traveller and spread the healthy values of sharing and conviviality, so deeply rooted in Hawaiian culture.

She was diagnosed with cancer in 1983 but did not relax her advocacy of the ethos of surfing nor reduce her number of world tours. Rell Sunn died in 1998, but she was so influential a teacher and such a loving person that her memory will always be treasured by surfers the world over.

Lisa Andersen:
surfing and parity

In spite of egalitarian Polynesian traditions, women's place in the professional surfing world was limited to just watching from the beach (as surfwidows) and getting a suntan. Freida Zamba or Wendy Botha were indeed world champions, three times apiece, but the difference in level and especially the popularity of surfing have always weighed things in favour of men, and overwhelmingly so. In fact it does not seem out of order to ask if surfers are macho.

By controlling the women's circuit of the 1990s and by her extremely radical approach to the sport, Lisa Andersen was able to repress these sexist assumptions and to change the conventions of the Pro Tour.

Lisa was a native of Ormond Beach, Florida and soon came up against her family's preference for education over surfing. Yet when she was 16 she decided to move to the west coast (Huntington Beach) in order to compete against the pick of the national and international elite with one aim in mind: to become world champion.

Divided between free surf and competitive events Lisa Andersen found it difficult to achieve consistent results. However, directly after the birth of her daughter in 1993, she realised her exceptional capabilities and things changed immediately. She won her first world title in 1994. In 1995 she became the second woman surfer in history (40 years of media coverage) to appear on the cover of the sacrosanct *Surfer Magazine*. In 1996 and 1997 she achieved awesome results by opting out of the women's Tour and entering official trials, in which she beat several male surfers, who acknowledged her as their equal. She became the first female pro surfer to win four world titles in a row and thus entered the Valhalla of international surfing.

But her influence on modern surfing was not limited to competitions. In the early 90s she helped create and develop a 100 per cent feminine brand: *Roxy* (by Quiksilver). In less than five years the women's market came to represent 15 per cent of the annual turnover for surfwear worldwide and most of the major brands developed several versions of a women's collection.

Today, between the birth of her second child and her work as coordinating officer of the ASP, Lisa still takes part in the main Pro Tour competitions. Many try to imitate her form and radical technique and she is quick to acknowledge that the level of women's surfing has advanced considerably over the last ten years.

Lisa is an infinitely versatile surfer and a most attractive mother. Her many successes will always ensure her a place in the history of modern surfing.

The surfer–globetrotter's guide

Not to touch on the theme of travel when talking about surfing would be a crime. Since its origins surfing has been intimately associated with travel. Nearly 80 per cent of the globe's surface is made up of oceans and seas; therefore the territory forming the surfer's field of expression is much more extensive than that of the skier, for example.

In the 1960s, Bruce Brown's first film *Endless Summer* perfectly defined the spirit of surfing: the quest for the perfect wave, following the summer from one hemisphere to another, and the taste for discovery and adventure. The film had a stupendous impact. It was the catalyst for the modern roving surfing community. From that point on, and thanks to new means of communication (planes, cars, mobile phones, the Internet), all destinations around the globe have become easily accessible and can be reached at an ever lower cost.

Over and above the wave pure and simple, each spot you go in search of has its history, its particular flavours, and its heroes.

You can surf on the seas and oceans of 5 continents! Welcome to planet surf.

Malibu

Situated to the north of the beaches of Los Angeles, for some considerable time the long stretch of the Malibu break has been the epicentre of Californian and world surfing fashions and trends. This regular point break, discovered by Tom Blake, is still one of the supreme locations for longboarding.

Pipeline

For nearly 30 years, this 'left-hander' reef of the North Shore (Oahu, Hawaii) has been the most hardcore wave for committed, if not reckless, surfers. A real pilgrimage for collectors of serious thrills, every winter this becomes the scene of incredible surfing sessions. Gerry Lopez is one of its masters. There is also Pipeline's equally legendary 'right-hander' twin: Backdoor.

Waimea

The symbolic icon of the North Shore, for a long time Waimea was considered to be the ultimate wave for bigwave riding. Every one of its stories has become part of its legendary history. It is the site of the Eddie Aikau Contest, one of the most dangerous waves for 'bigwave' surfing and a challenge for every bigwave rider.

Steamer Lane

Steamer Lane presents a series of left and right peaks and is situated to the north of Santa Cruz. It is the symbolic wave location of Northern California. Cold waters, floating seaweed, seals and white sharks are the gnarly ingredients of a reference index for hotdogging or great roller waves.

Sunset

This famous North Shore 'right-hander' is a technical wave with a fluctuating line up, mainly at takeoff. It is powerful and typically Hawaiian, an essential challenge for 'gigantic' wave surfers.

Jeffrey's Bay

Portrayed in Bruce Brown's film, *Endless Summer,* this long, cold and rocky South African (Cape St. Francis) 'right-hander' is the absolute ideal for every surfer in the world. All that goes to make up surfing comes together here in idyllic and natural harmony.

Kirra

A long 'right-hander' of rocks, this Australian wave offers heaps of fast sections. This is a real paradise for any regular (natural) surfer, tube practice is traditional, and this is the domain of Wayne 'Rabbit' Bartholomew.

Uluwatu

This long 'left-hander' reef, at the southern point of the island of Bali, Indonesia, has a special mystical quality. For a long time it was considered to be the initiation stretch for the roving surfer. Together with its neighbours, Padang-Padang, Bingin and Nusa Dua it remains a valuable provider of exoticism and tubes.

Tavarua

The discovery of Tavarua, Fiji, introduced the new era of boat-trips. This is a long, fast and tubular 'left-hander' with often-perfect surfing conditions. With warm waters, frequent swells and luxuriant marine flora and fauna, Tavarua is the ideal destination for surfers starved of exoticism.

Teahupoo

This 'left-hander' of coral reef entered into history in 2000 with the Laird Hamilton towed wave, nicknamed Millennium. Though more powerful, hollow, and intense it resembles its mythical cousin, Pipeline. In just a few years it has become a challenging wave in a glorious setting.

Nias

The wave of Lagundi, on Nias Island, Indonesia, is a long, coral reef 'right-hander'. Tubular and regular, isolated from civilisation, it belongs to the tradition of surreally dreamlike waves and is a paradise for every regular surfer in the world.

Saint-Leu

Kept a secret by local surfers for a long time, this long and regular Reunion 'left-hander' is the pearl of the Indian Ocean. With warm waters, multicoloured coral and a creole atmosphere you have all the ingredients to ensure that Saint Leu is entered in the directory of world-class waves.

Jaws

This powerful 'right-hander' is located on Maui, Hawaii, and is the worldwide shop-window for tow-in. This is a permanent scene of outstanding sessions, and the favourite playground of Laird Hamilton and his team. The cliff forms a natural cirque and offers an almost unique panorama.

Mundaka

This long, regular and tubular 'left-hander' is the pride of Spanish surfers. Between a romantic setting and the ocean's power, Mundaka is the reference index of European waves and a must-see for all globetrotting surfers.

Tresles

Two peaks, Lower and Upper, share the limelight on this San Clemente spot. Apart from the quality of the waves, Tresles is the home of all the most eccentric Californian trends (aerials, tricks, and reverses). This is where numerous champions such as the Fletcher family, the Beschen brothers and Matt Archbold started off.

Puerto Escundido

A beach-break on the Mexican west coast, Puerto Escundido is a series of powerful and deep peaks perfect for dedicated surfers. With its warm waters and a festive atmosphere Puerto is one of the planet's most beautiful beach-breaks.

Bell's Beach

This long 'right-hander' has a worldwide reputation and has been the scene of a series of fiercely competitive encounters. Less publicised nowadays, but very historic, it remains one of the treasures of the Australian coastline.

How does it work?

Although man first took to surfboards several centuries ago, technical progress has transformed the styles and techniques of modern surfing so radically that the surfer now has a totally different scope for style and technical development. At the beginning of the 20th century surfing meant just riding on and following the wave. Since the early 1970s and the appearance of the thruster (a surfboard with three fins), however, a much more exciting range of movements has become available, allowing the surfer to choose from a series of increasingly acrobatic and aerial manoeuvres.

The shape of the board plays an essential part in the development of technique and has undergone various changes over time. Here are a few photographs summarising the different stages of shaping a surfboard. Put on your mask and step into the workshop!

❶ The raw clark foam (polyurethane)

Since the advent of clark foam (polyurethane foam) the shape of the surfboard is formed in several stages, beginning with the raw clark foam. A mask must be worn as protection against the resinous fumes and vapours and the dust produced by sanding.

❷ Measurements and pre-cutting

The shaper determines the outline of the future surfboard, starting with the raw foam. All the measurements of rocker, size, width and thickness enable him to cut the foam roughly to the desired proportions with the help of a planer or sander (Photo by Loulou Barland).

❸ The shape

This is the most delicate and crucial stage of making a surfboard. The shape emerges from the blank as the result of precise sanding and planing and shows the future basic structure, or 'skeleton', of the surfboard (Photo by Mike Diffendorfer). The relationship between the shaper and surfer is supremely important. How the shape is defined depends on the taste, technique, height and weight of the surfer. Here, Sébastien Saint-Jean closely follows the experienced hands of Eric Arakawa (Photo by Sébastien Saint-Jean, Eric Arakawa).

❹ Glassing (glass laminating)

Once the shape is finished, the next operation involves methodically spreading a sheet of fibreglass over the board. Once it has been saturated with resin (polyester or epoxy), it hardens and sticks to the foam so that when it dries the surfboard is waterproof. The shaper decides when to apply a new layer of resin after the first layer of film-resin: glassing gives the surfboard a uniformly smooth texture (Photo by Thierry Domenech).

❺ Shaping machines

Using precise specifications, the Barland is a French invention able to shape blocks of foam in succession, and to allow for curvature. It is an ideal device for reproducing a cult model.

❻ Waxing

Before the board enters the water, it needs the final touch: waxing. This is a veritable ritual before each session. This minute amount of paraffin has anti-slip properties to prevent the surfer slipping on the board.

Made by **surfers** for **surfers**

From Tom Blake to Bob Simmons, by way of Gard Chapin or the illustrious Hawaiian forebears of modern waveriders, many surfers have been their own shapers. The surfing community was marginalised by the consumer society until the 1970s and had no real economic influence. Admittedly, several craft brands flourished after the war, but the surfing business remained anonymous and almost clandestine.

These small artisan workshops gradually developed their activities and in the fullness of time became the major enterprises we know today. Before becoming general producers, Quiksilver, Billabong and Oxbow began their businesses in surfwear; Rip Curl and O'Neill started by making wetsuits, and Rusty was the shape specialist.

These brands were players in the economic boom of the 1980s. They diversified their production and soon occupied all sectors of the surfing market. Today they aspire to compete with the main sportswear brands such as Nike or Adidas.

NOR CAL
surf shop
pedro point pacifica

Closely linked to the rise of professional surfing, the development of these brands lavished new financial means on competitive surfers. By the end of the 80s the 'top 16' surfers were actually able to live by their sport. The signing of the contract between Tom Caroll and Quiksilver (one million dollars for three years) heralded this change. Still a long way from receiving salaries like those of tennis players, footballers and basketball players, professional surfers like Wayne 'Rabbit' Bartholomew, Wayne Lynch and Martin Potter were nevertheless assured a future in the surfing industry.

As competitive surfers gradually reached a degree of financial independence, Christian Fletcher, the first professional free surfer, introduced another trend. The brands paid and promoted riders like Archbolt and Donavan Frankenreiter outside the traditional competition circuit because the values of freedom, which they stood for, were real marketing assets. For modern society however surfing is more than a fashion phenomenon. It is also a spiritual state, which becomes apparent in the form of a search for pleasure and a pronounced taste for travel and wide open spaces. Modern surfing is a powerful means of communication and a widely cited pastime whenever there is mention of nature, freedom or pleasure-seeking. It is hardly surprising it has found a place of its own in the western treasury of financial and media resources.

'Made by surfers for surfers' admirably expresses the respect for ecological ethics and values maintained by the surfing community, and stigmatises all the strategic gambles and ideologies of the third millennium.

The relationship between
man and nature

The British painter, Francis Bacon, said that man dominates nature only by domesticating it. This idea perfectly describes the bonds between the surfer and his environment: the ocean. Even before he masters nature, scarcely a legitimate aim anyway, man should learn to know and respect it. Knowledge of the seas, the wind's direction, the currents and the seasons is the very essence of surfing. Contrary to a number of forms of technical progress, surfing culture does not wish to harm nature, the very area in which it takes place. Coastal development and the explosion of seaside tourism are assaults on ecology and therefore on the practice of surfing. The building of marinas and sea walls destroys surfing spots and their history decays with them.

Nowadays it is not mere chance that advertisers love to associate the healthy values of surfing with a more or less fictitious ecological concern. In the collective unconscious, the surfer and the ocean enjoy an almost filial relationship. The surfer rides the wave and mixes instinct and technique: he is at one with nature.

Finally, the acceleration of climate change, international political inconsistencies (the *Prestige* oil tanker disaster) and the pollution of rivers have persuaded surfers to unite in order to combat anti-ecological deviancy.

Opposite page top and bottom: *Throughout the world, the accelerating rate of climatic disorder, international political inaction (e.g. the disaster caused by the oil-tanker Prestige) and river pollution are reasons why surfers co-operate in attempts to combat the anti-ecological deviations of modern economic systems.*

Surfrider Foundation

Surfrider Foundation was founded in 1985, thanks to Glen Hening and Tom Pratte. Its role is to give the world's surfers the means to fight against the depredations of our civilisation, vis-à-vis nature. A civil, non-profit making organisation open to all, the Surfrider Foundation has two methods of intervention: prevention and action.

Its interest in and deep awareness of the ocean enabled the surfing community to recognise the damaging effects of industrialisation on the eco-system well before its urban counterparts. The systematic discharge of hydrocarbons on to beaches, climatic changes and the adverse effects of El Nino are all offences against which the Surfrider Foundation campaigns and which it exposes around the world. The foundation convenes meetings, organises educational initiatives in schools, cleans beaches and pursues other effective activities. Well-publicised and timely actions like these help to unite like-minded people around the world. Monitoring of coastal waters and the holding of mass demonstrations herald a new trend: that of concerted interventions and activities to increase awareness.

In view of the increase in maritime disasters and the degradation of the world's climatic system, Surfrider Foundation is the fitting contribution of the planet's surfers to that which they hold so dear: the health of the ocean.

Right-hand page: *In view of the growing number of disasters at sea and the increasing deterioration of the world's climatic system, the surfers of the world have established the Surfrider Foundation in an attempt to protect the oceans about which they feel so passionately.*

Surfing, whether as a sport or an ancient art, has been able to adapt to the cultural developments of civilisation. It had almost disappeared in the early 20th century and its golden age is linked to the personality of its greatest ambassador, Duke Kahanamoku. In the present-day international context, having been marginalised if not totally excluded, surfing has come to symbolise freedom, pleasure and travel.

More than the sport itself, it is the spirit of surfing that has enabled it to explode economically and to become so universally popular. The surfing community passionately supports ecological ethics and values and is becoming increasingly involved in the struggle against pollution. Quite apart from the campaigns of the Surfrider Foundation, every surfer on the planet is committed to the defence of his wave, his coast and his ocean. That is also part of the spirit of surfing.

Surfing terminology

	manoeuvre	equipment	conditions	surfspeak	definition
aerial	•				taking off from the lip of the wave, landing on the wave face, and continuing
ailerons		•			fitted below the surfboard for turns and stability
anti-cyclone			•		climatic phenomenon without wind (opp.: depression)
ASP					Association of Surfing Professionals: international surfing organisation
backside				•	also backhand: surfing with one's back to the wave
beach break			•		wave breaking on a sandy beach
boat trip			•		moving from one island to another
bodyboard		•			small polyurethane board for riding a wave in a prone or drop-knee stance
bodysurf			•		riding the wave without a surfboard
bottom turn	•				turn at the bottom of the wave face
cover up	•				also shampooing; moving one's head under the crest of the wave
crossshore			•		wind across the wave
curl				•	the heart of the breaking wave
cutback	•				double turn on the face of the wave, taking the surfer back to the power centre
depression			•		climatic phenomenon favouring the creation of a swell in the sea
egg		•			type of surfboard used for small waves
exostosis				•	bony projection obstructing surfer's middle-ear cavity, caused by cold water
fish		•			a type of surfboard for small waves
flat			•		no swell, quite calm
floater	•				moving the board on to a breaking wave then freefalling with it
foam		•			soft polyurethane foam for making surfboards
free surf	•				surfing without regard to outcome
frontside				•	position of surfer descending while facing the wave
glassy			•		calm, smooth sea with little or no wind
goofy foot				•	surfing with right foot forward, left foot to rear
grip		•			anti-slip rubber patch instead of wax
gun		•			long, narrow waveboard for big waves
He'e Nalu				•	Hawaiian term for surfing
hotdogging	•				surfing technique for small waves
impact zone			•		zone of turbulence where a wave breaks most heavily
inside			•		on the shore side of a breaking wave; inside a tube; the rail closest to the wave face
layback	•				moving below the crest of the wave with one's back to the wave
leash		•			cord attaching the surfboard to the surfer's foot
left				•	also 'lefthander': a wave breaking from left to right when seen from the shore
lift				•	shaping technique
lineup				•	area just outside a break, or point, where a wave begins to break
longboard		•			large surfboard for riding big or small waves
New School				•	new generation of 90s surfers with styles influenced by skateboarding and snowboarding
normal foot				•	also natural foot: left foot forward, right foot back
nose		•			front part of a surfboard
offshore			•		wind blowing from the land out to sea (ideal)
onshore			•		wind blowing from the sea on to the land (not ideal)

	manoeuvre	equipment	conditions	surfspeak	definition
outrigger		•			traditional Polynesian craft
outside			•		wave breaking far out; area beyond the area of impact
paddleboard		•			large surfboard introduced by Tom Blake for lifesaving
païpo		•			Hawaiian term for the forerunner of the bodyboard
point break			•		wave breaking on point (or headland) and refracted around it
priority				•	a surfer taking off right inside a wave has priority over other surfers
rail		•			edge of a surfboard
rash vest		•			lycra T-shirt to protect skin from wetsuit rubbing or from solar radiation
re-entry	•				surfing up into the lip of a breaking wave, then descending with it
reverse	•				180 degree manoeuvre
right				•	also 'righthander': a wave breaking from right to left when seen from the shore
rocker				•	the curve in a surfboard when seen side-on
roller	•				turning at the top of the wave
section				•	breaking portion or segment of a wave
session				•	single uninterrupted surfing occasion
set				•	series or group of waves
shape				•	make a surfboard
shooting				•	taking a wave
shore break			•		wave that breaks close into the shore
shortboard		•			small surfboard
shortie		•			wetsuit for warm, summer surfing
single		•			surfboard with one fin
snapback	•				a more extreme form of cutback or turn on the face of the wave
spot				•	surfing location
street				•	synonym for trendy and popular, borrowed from skateboarding
surfing				•	riding waves
surfcamps				•	holiday camps for surfers, located near surfing spots
surfriding				•	surfing
surfshops				•	stores selling surfing gear and surfwear
surfwear				•	surfing clothing
surfwidow				•	neglected partner of enthusiastic surfer
swell			•		movement of a wave from creation (depression) to the point of breaking on the shore
tail				•	rear of the surfboard
takeoff	•				starting to ride the wave
tandem				•	artistic waveriding by two surfers
thruster		•			a surfboard with three fins (traditional since the end of the 70s)
tow-in	•				surfing having been towed out to sea
trials					qualification events before the main event
tricks	•				manoeuvres inspired by skateboarding and/or snowboarding
trip				•	surfing journey
tube	•				inside of a hollow wave
tuberiding	•				surfing the inside of a hollow wave
twin-fin		•			a surfboard with two fins
wax		•			a mixture of paraffin and beeswax to prevent slipping on the board
webcam		•			Internet cam
wetsuit		•			snug-fitting neoprene suit to keep surfers warm

Further information

Bibliography

G. Lynch, M. Gault-Williams & W.K. Hoopes:
The Uncommon Journey of a Pioneer Waterman
(The Croul Family Foundation, 2001)
M. Gault-Williams: *Legendary Surfers, 'a Definitive
History of Surfing's Culture and Heroes'*, vols. 1-4, 1993–
2004 (as e-books at www.legendarysurfers.com)
A. Colas: *The World Stormrider Guide* (Low Pressure
Publications, 2001)

Internet sites

Surfersvillage.com
Surfreport.com
Surflink.com
Surfinfo.com
Stormsurf.com
Baliwaves.com
Transworldsurf.com
Surfsystem.co.uk
Surfline.com
Viewsurf.com
Wannasurf.com
Aspworldtour.com
Legendarysurfers.com
Surfrider.org
Surfer.com

Filmography*

(Hollywood productions)
Gidget (1959)
Beach Party (1963)
Endless Summer (1964)
Bikini Beach (1964)
The Horror of Party Beach (1964)
Muscle Beach Party (1964)
Surf Party (1964)
Ride the Wild Surf (1964)
The Girls on the Beach (1965)
Wild on the Beach (1965)
How to Stuff a Wild Bikini (1965)
The Beach Girls and the Monster (1965)
Beach Blanket Bingo (1965)
Murph the Surf (1975)
Big Wednesday (1978)
Apocalypse Now (1979)
North Shore (1982)
Fast Times at Ridgemont High (1982)
Surf II (1984)
Surf Nazis Must Die (1987)
Point Break (1991),
In God's Hands (1998)
Blue Crush (2002)
Die Another Day (2002)
Billabong Odyssey (2004)

*Films that have become cult movies for surfers are
in bold type